DSM-K for Kepele

Jolie Pataki, MD

For additional knowledge and a deeper understanding of Yiddish words, feel free to explore:
https://www.hebrew4christians.com/Glossary/Yiddish_Words/yiddish_words.html

LCCN: 2025917434

Paperback ISBN: 978-1-968966-49-2

Hardcover ISBN: 978-1-968966-50-8

Dedication

Dedicated to my soulmate, Mom,
who taught me much of what follows,
and of course her actual mate, Dad.

(The next one will be dedicated to my kids and CJ.)

About the Author

Several books have been written about "talking to" or "talking back to" psychotropic medications and whatnot. This one is about diagnosis, using perhaps the most accurately descriptive language ever spoken: Yiddish. I have been a psychiatrist for more than 30 years and a Jew for more than 60 (despite my youthful looks!). So, as my alter-ego, Dr. Fackacta, I have put together my take on descriptive experiences in this field of mental health.

Introduction

Mental health characterization and insights are often changing. Our field is a descriptive one that struggles to assert clear, concrete diagnoses. Psychiatric labels have come and gone, but when there wasn't even a diagnosis available, Yiddish could almost invariably offer an applicable word or phrase to succinctly capture the essence of even the most 'difficult to diagnose' patient. There is no reference to this in the Glossary of Culture-Bound Syndromes within our current psychiatric lexicon. Some have observed that if you get 10 psychiatrists in a room to evaluate one patient, you will end up with 10 different diagnoses! While our field is closely aligned with neurology, we used to joke that psychiatry is all treatment and no diagnosis, while neurology is all diagnosis with no treatment. Medical science in both fields has evolved but this is still a humorous depiction. And while we are still on the topic of humor, how many psychiatrists does it take to change a lightbulb? Only one, but the lightbulb has to want to change....

Earlier DSMs included five Axes that described not only the major diagnoses but included additional dimensions of personality disorders, stressors, medical problems and overall level of functioning. I believe these are helpful in characterizing the whole patient so I included Axis II (Personality Disorders) and a sprinkling of medical references. So here is the DSM-K (for Kepele).

This is a new (and quite possibly improved!) way to classify and refer to our bread-and-butter, with a bit of "oy". One of the fathers of psychiatry, surely at least the begetter of Analysis, Sigmund Freud, happened to be Jewish; there seems to be a rather large number of his (our) brethren who have followed in his therapeutic footsteps. (It occurs to me that most of his insights probably came from his Mameleh, Amalie.)

Continuing research, observation and consensus may further refine diagnoses but to change more than five thousand years' worth of tradition would be a shanda!

Cautionary Statement

These descriptors are meant to assist (and amuse) the clinician (whether or not they or their patient is Jewish), but should not be considered absolute. In some cases, epidemiologic information such as gender differences or effective treatments are noted. These diagnoses have definitely NOT been arrived at by expert consensus; can you imagine a gaggle of Jewish mothers in one room, all expounding on THEIR (respective) points of view? Nonetheless, the proper understanding and use of these terms requires specialized clinical training, not to mention chutzpah, that affords the clinician both a body of knowledge and clinical skills. They are not exhaustive (but why would anyone need more?). They help define what has most assuredly been noticed and criticized by any Jewish mother worth her latkes.... This nomenclature does not completely jive with the likes of the WHO or the ICD, but who knows, that could happen, nu? Maybe... next year... in Jerusalem. Oh, and these are not to be used for legal purposes, despite your brother-in-law being a lawyer. When you're done reading, be sure to pass it on to your mother, but please turn on the light for her first!

Use of the Manual

Shtik, we all have, but one must learn proper interviewing techniques as well as acquire a discerning ear for nuances contained in responses. A good opening line to get the patient talking could be, "And, what's YOUR shpiel?"

Now, just because a prospective patient might answer a question posed to him/her with another question, it by no means invalidates said response. In fact, it probably adds credibility. In addition, tone of voice adds great meaning, as does context. One can certainly consider the many intimations of the word "oy": "Oh" and "Oh So Much More!"

So nu, let's get to it already!

Axis I

1) Disorders Diagnosed in Infancy, Childhood, or Adolescence (not MY kid, kina-hora)

There is a great deal of variation in how and when individuals develop. There are certain expectations of communication, behavior and functioning. However, deviation from average expectations can be a problem. The trick is to distinguish between illness and mishegos. This is not so easy. Either one can give you tsouris, but treatment? Oy vey!

Michering Disorder (Dysfunctional expressive communication)

Difficulty in understanding what the little tatele is fussing about, leading adults to repeatedly ask, "Vus iz dus?"

Fershtay Disorder (Learning Disability or Apparent Receptive Communication Disorder)

Often manifested by the inability to understand spoken language, no matter how LOUD it is spoken. This must not otherwise be accounted for by the common phenomenon of several people trying to speak at once, which can mimic this illness.

Nudnik Disorder

Behavioral dyscontrol, whereby the child does not follow directions despite admonitions to do so, becomes more than a nuisance, realizing (quite compassionately) that it comes from the in-laws' side of the family.

Treatment: You should have married the one I picked out for you.

(There is an increased risk among siblings of patients with this disorder.)

Add-Hock Disorder

Excessive, repetitive, recurrent, redundant nagging.

Selective Mutism

Never been reported.

2) Dementia and Cognitive Disorders

There are many ways to describe levels of intellectual dysfunction, with different origins, some acute and some chronic. Sometimes medical conditions underlie these disturbances; sometimes not. Who could know these things? Sadly, these afflictions are all too common in alta-cockers.

Fartummelt Disorder

Acute confusion, from any origin, most often due to poor planning during holiday family get-togethers. It is often temporary and resolves on its own with supportive treatment only.

Farblunget Disorder

Acquired difficulty with short-term memory and executive function. Includes disappointment that your son-in-law didn't become an executive or win a Nobel Prize. No known treatment.

Amnestic Disorders

Characterized by deficits in recall of details of past events, particularly social interactions including explicit details of previous conversations. It seems to be genetically Y-linked as it has never been reported in females.

3) Disorders Arising From Known Medical Conditions

Complaining about a suspected medical disorder is probably as effective a precipitant as actually having it.

Kvetch Disorder

Repetitive verbalization of complaints that are presumed to originate from multiple medical maladies but probably aren't.

Kishke Disorder

Perpetual concerns and expectations but minimal evidence of medical dysfunction, often focused on abdominal complaints and may lead to more medical illness. This is further distinguished from the preceding disorder by much less verbalization.

Ibbledick Disorder

General malaise that seems to occur as a vicious cycle with aggravation, agitation, anxiety and not enough knaidlach in the chicken soup (which wasn't as good as yours, anyway).

Shmerts Disorder

Chronic pain syndrome, with pathognomonic krekhtsn: "THIS hurts," "THAT hurts," (and you thought KVETCHING was the only way to complain of pain!).

4) Disorders Arising from Chazeray Abuse

Manischewitz Abuse Drinking Disorder (MADD)

Too much partying (even with the blessing of the rebbe). Luckily, a person will usually become hyperglycemic before becoming farshnoshket. Real umglicks end up as both.

5) Psychotic Disorders

Meshugenah

A bissel crazy. Symptoms can be classified as positive (though what could be positive about them?), such as delusions or elaborate made-up stories – bubbamaisa; or simply nothingness – bubkes. Either way, there is significant dysfunction. These symptoms can vary greatly, with most patients becoming farmisht. There can be a whole megillah of complex symptoms, as their illnesses are a farshlepte krenk.

Shmontes Disorder

Thought process where seykhel is replaced by nonsense and narishkeit.

Tsedrayt Disorder

Delusional symptoms such that a nebbish might think he or she is a real macher or maven. Some have complained that they are possessed by a dybbuk (although modern science has proved this wrong, a dip in the Mikvah couldn't hurt).

Shreklach Disorder

Acute, paranoid state of fixed, false belief characterized by fear of turning into a big green bulvan.

Folie-A-Jew

When the whole mishpokhe is crazy.

Beshert Disorder

Non-bizarre delusion that another person, maybe of higher status, is in love with and wants to marry this individual.

6) Mood Disorders

There is a wide spectrum of mood disorders, with the two extremes diametrically opposed (such as one side of the machetunum vs. the other). However, there can be some mixing of the two. Mixed states themselves can be confusing. They are episodic and there is usually a precipitating event that can be identified. Precipitants are often related to anticipation of approaching yuntif.

Major Dershlogn Disorder (MOD)

Characterized by extreme sadness and vegetative symptoms such as poor energy and dragging oneself through the day.

Verklempt Affective Disorder (VAD)

Excessive emotional reactions which are characterized by episodes of naches alternating with veytik. During the naches phase, there are associated symptoms of constant kibbitzing, over-the-top chutzpah, and excessive buying of chatchkes. Inflated sense of self-concept masquerading as a maven can be observed. During the veytik phase, sadness is accompanied by feeling like a nudnik, schliemiel, schlamazel, schmegegge, schmo, and generally nebbishik. If it progresses to the degree of total mieskeitik, or to prevent plotzing, hospitalization may be warranted.

Feh Disorder

A less severe, chronic state of sadness characterized by feeling that everything is schlock, with a loss of interest in enjoyable activities such as schmoozing and shmying.

7) Noshing Disorders

Gefilte Disorder

Eating so much carp and/or pike on Passover, that one becomes too fillte.

Non-gefilte Disorder

Eating so much other food on Passover that one still becomes too fillte.

8) Shpilkes Disorders

These disorders represent varying types of anxiety.

Plotz Attacks (With or Without Agoraphobia)
Sudden attacks or episodes of anxiety accompanied by shvitzing and spritzing.

Gevalt Anxiety Disorder (GAD)
General, free-floating anxiety that leads to continually asking for reassurance.

Tsouris
Chronic low-level nervous energy that leads to constant motion, especially hand-wringing.

Potchking Disorder
Either intrusive obsessions or compulsions that lead to repetitive, useless behaviors that lead to absolutely gornisht, but are irrepressible. These behaviors cannot be easily kiboshed or kaput.

Post Traumatic Shlepping Disorder (PTSD)

Carrying the baggage of past traumatic experiences and associated symptoms that recur and lead to significant disability. This usually results from severe trauma but has been reported as a sequela to major shopping sprees.

9) Shluffen Disorders

Nisht Shluffen Nicht-time

Inability to fall asleep – frequently evolves due to sleeping with a schnorrer loudly snoring too close to you.

10) Impulse Control Disorders

Intermittent Zetz Disorder (IZD)

This is defined by several discrete episodes of failure to resist aggressive impulses to hit people, grossly out of proportion to any precipitating psychosocial stressors.

Kipahmania

This is characterized by the recurrent failure to resist impulses to steal yarmulkes not needed for personal use or monetary value.

11) Disorders of Sexuality

It's a mitzvah to have sex on Friday nights. How could this be an illness?

12) Somatoform Disorders

Conversion Disorder

Having the urge to marry a shiksa or a shaygetz.

Pupick Disorder

Having a distorted view of one's body, at times leading to recurrent attempts at correcting perceived deficit. This has been seen mostly in young females manifested by repeatedly wearing extraordinarily short shirts, exposing their entire midriff and thinking this was appropriate.

Lokh in Kop

Disorder usually affecting parents of females afflicted with Pupick Disorder, who fear that they may need or already have holes in their cerebral cortex.

Axis II

Personality/Adjustment Disorders

Glitsch (Personality) Disorders

These disorders are characterized by shtik and shlep: one's personal style of doing things which are mieskeit- or zeeskeit-adaptive, combined with the weight/burdens of excessive emotional baggage, respectively.

Forbissena Cluster

Self-explanatory but could lead to a bitter pill to swallow.

Keit Cluster

Too much of the good (zeiskeits), the bad (mieskeits), and the bubkes.

Shuldik Cluster

Excessive guilt with persistent thoughts of shoulda-woulda-coulda.

Petchetch Cluster

Repeatedly making a tzimmes out of gornisht, frequent complaints of not having enough chatchkes and unrealistic expectations of self-gratification.

Klutz Cluster

Repeated tripping over things, especially excessive chatchkas.

Chutzpah Cluster

Even more self-explanatory.

Axis III

Medical Disorders

Trust me, leave these to your daughter, the doctor…

Axis IV

As if the disease itself wasn't enough, you had to make things worse?! These are the factors that exacerbate Axes I-III. These are itemized mishegos that contribute to the morbidity and mortality (God forbid!) of above mental health symptoms. This axis is fair game for any and all mishegos, including that which is caused by non-mishpohke.

www.ingramcontent.com/pod-product-compliance
Lightning Source LLC
Chambersburg PA
CBHW051253120626
46547CB00014B/1922